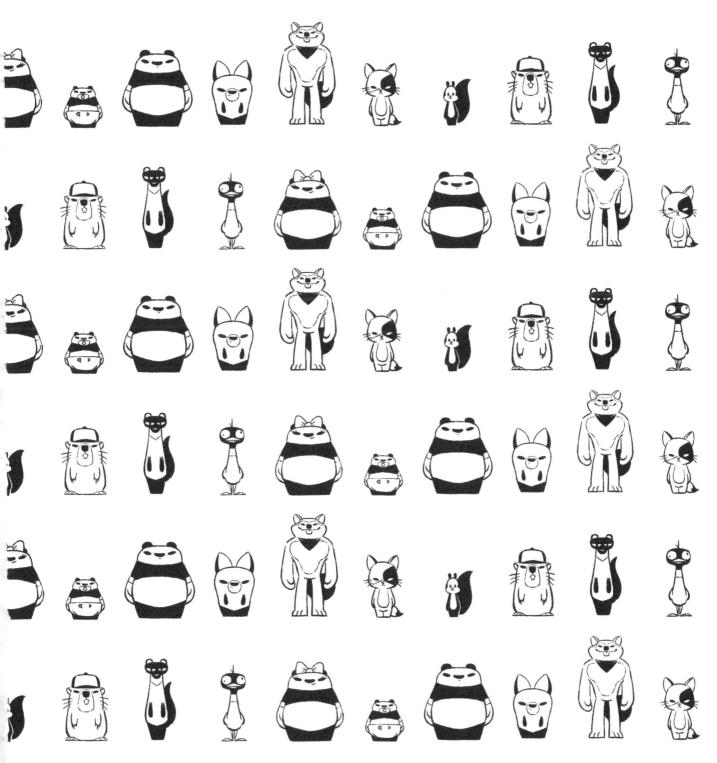

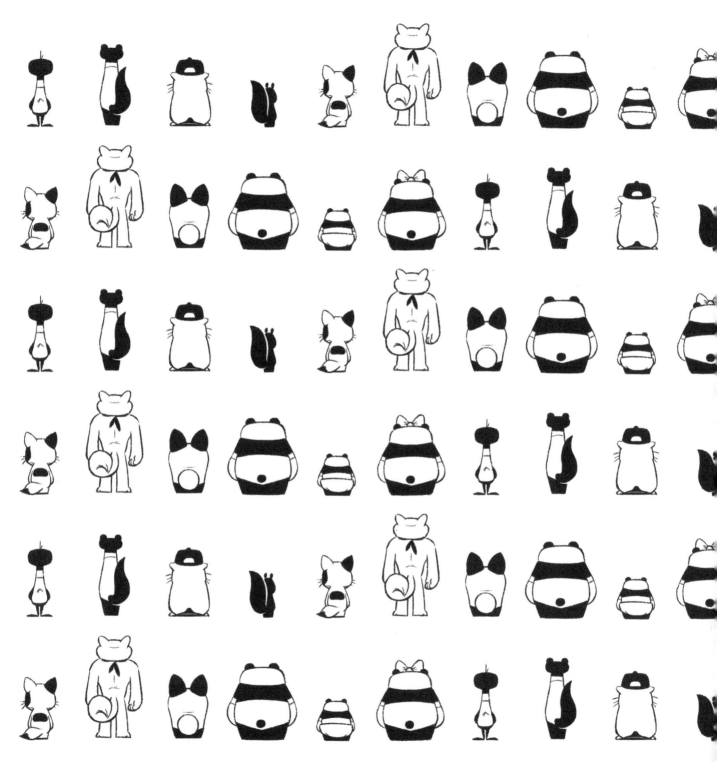

Pak

Petunia

Baby Jr.

Randy

Topher

Chimu

Nop

Summer

Buxton

Steve

To panda brothers and sisters

Panda is Still Fat and Other Panda Haikus | written and illustrated
by Nolen Lee

Summary: A collection of haikus and illustrations featuring Pak the
punching panda and his pals. Featuring Petunia Panda, Baby Jr. Panda,
Randy the red panda, Topher the Akita dog, Chimu the calico cat, Nop the
mallard duck, Summer the squirrel, Buxton the beaver, and Evil Steve
the yellow-throated marten (actually he's not Pak's friend).

Published by Punching Pandas, LLC.
First edition: June 2019
ISBN 978-0-578-53576-0
punchingpandas.com

Panda is **Still** Fat

and Other Panda Haikus

Made by Nolen Lee

Punching Pandas®

Panda is still fat

Must find a way to lose weight

Panda will find way

Self control is good

All things in moderation

Well... almost all things

Better one sharp blade

Than having many dull blades

Where did I put it?

Humility comes

When we know what we don't know

So, know no know, no?

The cup is half full

Or it can be half empty

Panda needs refill

The past is behind

And the future is ahead

Where is the present?

If a tree falls down

And panda does not hear it

Should panda still care?

One cannot see wind

But one can see what it moves

Wind likes to move trash

Some see shades of gray

Some also see black and white

Or some see panda

Peace is the answer

There is no room for fighting

There's just five letters

There are some pictures

That are worth a thousand words

Maybe not this one

23

26

When panda with wife

Feels like time is standing still

Maybe clock broken

A life companion

Will always be by your side

Unless there's a door

There is wise saying

"Happy wife makes happy life"

Wait, did wife write this?

A child's innocence

Cherish it for it is brief

This child is guilty

Enjoy the moment

For moments pass by quickly

Except this moment

The role of parents

Difficult but rewarding

When is the reward?

Timeless traditions

Bring young and old together

To do silly things

It is your birthday

A tasty cake made for you

It tastes good, I checked

Dog is a good friend

Dog will never leave panda

Oh look, a squirrel

Panda has to work

Cat is sitting on keyboard

Panda does not work

When doing business

The customer's always right

Except for this guy

Do not be rigid

Be like water in a cup

Unless it's frozen

An inspiration

Can come at any moment

Now's not a good time

When life gives lemons

Use them to make lemonade

This needs more sugar

A thousand-mile trip

Begins with a single step

Or a plane ticket

When there is a mess

We can all work together

And make it bigger

59

The light is brightest

In the darkest of hours

Hey, turn off your phone!

The brave explorer

Makes new paths where none have tread

Or where none come back

Leaders who are wise

Will listen to followers

And go in circles

Spring brings in the new

New life, new hope, and new love

And new allergies

Summer sun is bright

Its warm glow shines on us all

I need more sunscreen

Autumn signals change

A season of transition

To lousy weather

74

The soft winter snow

Covers hills in white blanket

I need real blanket

When you see beauty

Take moment to enjoy it

Can I eat it yet?

Talent is nurtured

There is no one born with it

Well, except for some

To be successful

One needs to set the bar high

Or lower the bar

There are no losers

Everyone is a winner

But we know who won

One's true character

How does one measure one's worth?

With a longer tape

Panda is not fat

Panda sits on a seesaw

Panda is still fat

Punching Pandas® was created by Nolen Lee who enjoyed drawing ever since growing up in Portland, Oregon, because there was nothing better to do. After graduating with a Masters in Engineering, he pursued art because he liked to make fake buildings instead of real ones. In 2018, he wrote "The Pandas is Fat," which many say is the best panda haiku book in the world, until the one you are reading right now. He is still married and is a father to a small rabid animal.

Check out the panda's first book. Available at a bookstore near or far away from you.

Visit panda and friends at
punchingpandas.com

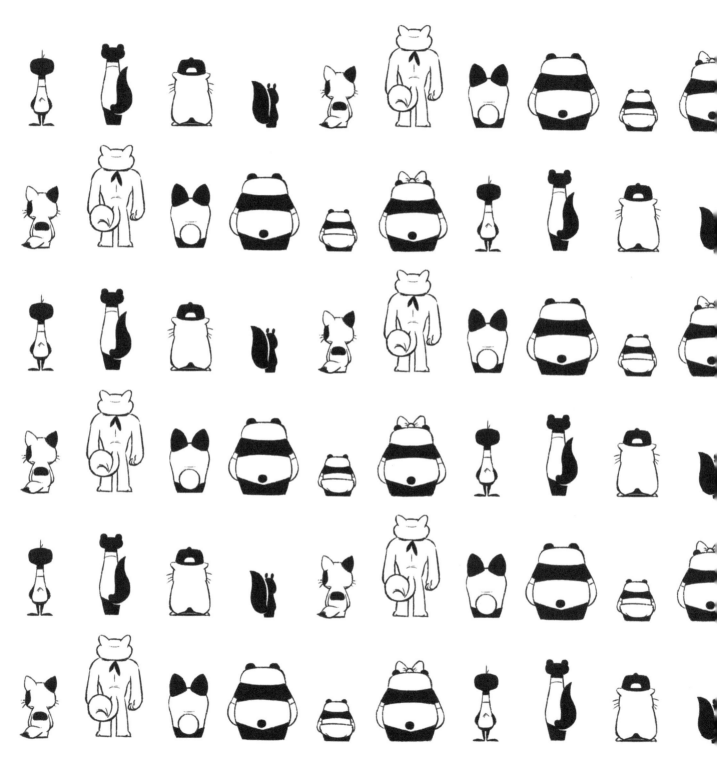

CPSIA information can be obtained
at www.ICGtesting.com
Printed in the USA
LVHW071031221222
735725LV00002B/4